FUN
FOR

C000077996

**By Brin Best
& Ken Dunn**

Cartoons:
Phil Hailstone

Published by:

Teachers' Pocketbooks
Laurel House, Station Approach,
Alresford, Hampshire SO24 9JH, UK
Tel: +44 (0)1962 735573
Fax: +44 (0)1962 733637
E-mail: sales@teacherspocketbooks.co.uk
Website: www.teacherspocketbooks.co.uk

*Teachers' Pocketbooks is an imprint of
Management Pocketbooks Ltd.*

All rights reserved. No part of this publication
may be reproduced, stored in a retrieval
system or transmitted in any form, or by any
means, electronic, mechanical, photocopying,
recording or otherwise, without the prior
permission of the publishers.

© Brin Best and Ken Dunn 2005.

This edition published 2005.

ISBN 1903776 65 1

British Library Cataloguing-in-Publication
Data – A catalogue record for this book is
available from the British Library.

Design, typesetting and graphics by Efex Ltd.
Printed in UK.

Contents

Introduction

If we've done our job properly, this will be the best £6.99 your school has ever spent. Our aim is to provide a book that will bring in **substantial funds** for your school on a **sustainable** basis. We're not talking about one-off successes or lucky breaks – the meat of our book introduces you to a model, and a set of principles and tools, that will help put your school's fundraising efforts on a really professional footing. This will bring long-term gains and allow you to get your fair share of the external funds available to schools.

When it comes to fundraising, schools fall into two broad groups – the 'haves' and the 'have nots'. But when you look beneath the surface, it's not an accident that the 'haves' seem to get all the success. They're successful because they have in place the systems they need to be successful and have developed the specific skills required to gain external funding. On top of that, they have a clear **vision** of where their fundraising is taking them.

Introduction

We've based this book around our **ten-step model** of successful fundraising.
This is inspired partly by our own fundraising experience and successes in the schools
we've worked in and supported over the last two decades, and partly by best practice
from the most effective schools in the UK.

In this era of tests, targets and myriad other education priorities, it's easy to lose sight
of what schools are for: providing high quality education for young people. This book
will help you to raise the funds you need to **extend** and **enrich** the education of the
students in your care. It is highly practical in that it suggests specific actions which will
take your work to the next level.

However, achieving fundraising success requires sustained effort over a considerable
time. There are no shortcuts that will bring you success overnight. Although there
are lots of hints and tips in the book, if you build these in to an overall **strategy**, then
the results will be so much more powerful.

Introduction

We've written this book with two main types of reader in mind:

1. **Senior managers** or **governors** wishing to set up systems that will enable their school to become effective at fundraising. To take forward the ideas in this book we recommend that you appoint a **fundraising coordinator** to oversee the work in your school, which by no means has to be a large financial investment. It is vital to provide a very clear brief for this person's work, built around a vision for the school with an indication of the scale of fundraising expected. This is where your leadership is needed.

2. People who have been given the role of **coordinating** or overseeing fundraising in their school and want to know where to begin. Our **ten-step model** in particular allows you to work through a step-by-step plan for devising an effective fundraising strategy. As you work through the book, however, you may realise that some things will need to change in your school before you can set to work properly.

Introduction

We're sometimes asked by people working in schools whether or not schools should be fundraising. The short answer is 'no'. In an ideal world the government would provide sufficient funds for every possible educational enhancement in our schools.

But of course we don't live in that ideal world, and neither does anyone else. No country has been able to fund education to this utopian level, so we have to accept that if we want to go above and beyond what is provided by the state then we need to look elsewhere for the funds.

Looking elsewhere for funds actually raises an exciting opportunity. As you look out to your local and wider communities for support, a magical thing happens. You realise the huge potential of working in partnership with your community to implement improvements or projects in your school that can change lives.

Introduction

We accept that **minor campaign fundraising** for specific projects or initiatives is as far as some of you want to go. Or indeed a general **modest increase** in the school budget would be perfectly acceptable. Perhaps you wish to increase staffing, or have a classroom you would like to refurbish?

'But I don't want to build an ambitious vision for my school - I just need some more money for everyday resources!'

There's much in the book to help you reach these goals, but we'd like to encourage you to be a bit more **ambitious** with your plans. Having visited some outstanding educational projects in schools across the country, we know the amazing impact these can have on young people and communities. We hope, when **the time is right** for you, you too will be inspired by these schools and build your own exciting vision.

Setting
the Scene

 Getting
Started

 The Ten-Step
Model

 Fundraising
in Action

 Monitoring
and
Evaluating

 Tools/Further
Information

Setting the Scene

A short history

External fundraising by state schools in this country can be split into **three** main phases:

1. **Pre-1980** – almost all schools were engaged in low-level fundraising activities, characterised by events such as fêtes and sponsored walks. This typically brought in up to a few thousand pounds annually in an opportunistic way.

2. **1980-1994** – a few schools became more professional in obtaining external funds. They organised minor campaigns aimed at bringing in sums up to £50,000. Most schools were still reliant on 'events'.

3. **1994-present** – more and more schools became aware of the potential to raise significant sums of money from external sources. Some mounted major campaigns for sums in excess of £50,000. This was fuelled by the introduction of the National Lottery and the specialist schools scheme. A few schools became highly professional at accessing funds, and appointed fundraising coordinators. Many schools, however, were still mainly reliant on 'events'.

How much money are schools raising?

The most recent comprehensive survey of school fundraising in the UK focused on state schools in England (DSC 2000). It found that:

- Schools in England were raising over £230 million a year from external sources
- Primary schools were raising £4,000 a year on average
- Secondary schools were raising £40,000 a year on average
- Special schools were raising almost £9,000 a year on average

The latest DfES figure suggests that state and independent schools are now raising over £1.5 billion between them.

The 'haves' and the 'have nots'

The figures for school fundraising hide the fact that in reality **some** schools are doing very well (raising more than £100,000 every year), whereas **most** schools are only raising small amounts (often less than £1,000). These are the funding 'haves' and 'have nots'.

It's interesting to consider whether you think your school is getting its fair share of this £230 million each year. The fact that you are reading this book probably indicates that it's not! But take heart, this book is designed to help you get a fairer share.

500 Children to Support & Teach

Three success stories

1. Royston High School, Barnsley, South Yorkshire

The arrival of a new head of geography and an application form from the educational charity Learning Through Landscapes (LTL) sparked a remarkable transformation in this comprehensive school in a former mining village in South Yorkshire.

The application form asked if there was any part of the school in need of a make-over. The head of geography had seen many inspiring landscapes on his travels and could only answer, 'Yes – the whole lot of it!' He formed an environment group and, with help from Barnsley Council's countryside planning department, 'greening' took place around the school entrances. Additional trees, shrubs and tools were acquired via a couple of bank-sponsored conservation awards and, spurred on by these successes, the group submitted a bid to LTL.

The geography teacher's vision centred around a courtyard of soggy grass. His idea was to create a micro-river system complete with waterfall, meanders, gorge and estuary. As the school was located in a former coal-mining village, he wanted to challenge the perception that energy just comes from black stuff in the ground, by powering the stream via renewable energy.

Three success stories

Royston High School, Barnsley, South Yorkshire (cont'd)

The idea alone triggered a £1,300 start-up grant from LTL, and many awards later, after hundreds of hours of community collaboration, the courtyard was complete. The creation of this unique hands-on resource was extremely powerful - and not just in terms of the wind turbine and solar panels employed! It demonstrated very forcefully to the whole community that change was possible in this financially-depressed area.

Now promoted to school development manager and excused some of the meetings that sap the life out of middle managers, the geography teacher set about tackling other areas of the school. Redirecting his time into fundraising was to prove invaluable. He gained several additional grants and awards, which brought about a transformation in many areas of the school. Not least was the creation of a multi-sports area, the envy of many a sports college. In total over £200,000 was raised for a wide range of projects.

Three success stories

2. Woodheys Primary School, Sale, Greater Manchester

A school governor and teaching assistant at this primary school set in train a series of highly creative events and projects that have put it at the forefront of education for sustainable development and raised tens of thousands of pounds.

The work began with an £800 award to paint colourful murals in the cloakrooms, a welcome opportunity for a school serving an area of considerable deprivation. Success led to further bids, which were rewarded by grants to create a tropical oasis garden and a host of environmental projects involving children. The PTA was then inspired to professionalise its own fundraising efforts, with a range of imaginative ideas, culminating in an 'auction of promises' which raised £3,000 in one night. The school replaced its time-consuming jumble sales by working with Bag 2 School (www.bag2school.com), an ethical organisation that gives schools cash for clothing.

The most recent event, a flower festival, saw the school stage a major fundraiser while also allowing the children to show their creative work to parents, carers and the wider community. TV gardener Jeff Turner chaired a gardeners' question time session, helping the school raise almost £2000 for its new outdoor classroom project.

Three success stories

3. Settle High School, North Yorkshire

During the mid-1990s an imaginative subject leader at this small rural comprehensive school successfully gained funding for a range of small projects. Encouraged by this, the headteacher created the post of development officer which allowed one hour per week of dedicated time for coordinating the school's fundraising activities. The school went on to win a string of regional and national awards for its imaginative curricular and extra-curricular work between 1996 and 2000, including prizes for an environment exchange, a science fair with local primary schools and the production of a Millennium Map of the town.

When the school mounted its campaign to become a technology college in 2001 the development officer was given a full day per week to focus on fundraising. The school community was hit hard by the foot and mouth crisis and fundraising was extremely challenging. However, in three terms over £50,000 in matched funding was raised. In June 2003 the school was successful in its bid to become a technology college and was awarded £450,000 in funding from the government.

What do these stories tell us?

These three stories are examples of real schools that have taken on the challenge of external fundraising and achieved remarkable results. As well as providing inspiration for your work they help to illustrate that:

- Major success is built on smaller successes, which in turn build confidence
- A determination to succeed can overcome seemingly insurmountable barriers to progress
- Successful fundraising does not only happen when a full-time member of staff is dedicated solely to the role – even a small time commitment can generate impressive results

In short, we believe that it's **always** worth committing time and resources to external funding, providing you follow a recognised model for success. Much of this book focuses on providing you with that model and helping you develop the knowledge and skills that will bring you success.

Things to consider

It's vital to begin by **reflecting** on a few key areas before beginning your fundraising work.

- Do the senior management team and governors have a clear desire to make fundraising a priority?
- Are other staff at your school ready and willing to take on the challenge?
- What is your school's experience of fundraising to date?
- What skills does your school already have that can be brought to bear?
- How will your community feel about any fundraising efforts?

Consider these questions carefully. As a school you need to **commit formally** to beginning your fundraising work. It will not come without its costs and sacrifices and, if you are going to be successful, you must be realistic about what will need to change. Is this the most appropriate time to take on the challenge?

The need for a whole-hearted effort

Once your school has formally committed to begin fundraising:

- The whole school community needs to know why the work has begun
- Time will need to be created for somebody to coordinate the work
- Meetings will need to take place
- The work needs to be monitored and evaluated
- You need to be patient as success will not come immediately

If any of these areas are neglected then your work will simply not be as effective as it could be. It should be given the same level of commitment as a curriculum development, and not be done in the scraps of time left over at the end of the week.

The future?

Won't it be a great day when our school has all the money it needs and the RAF has to hold a jumble sale to buy its new bomber?

Sign displayed in a primary school staffroom.

Setting
the Scene

 Getting
Started ◀

 The Ten-Step
Model

 Fundraising
in Action

 Monitoring
and
Evaluating

 Tools/Further
Information

Getting Started

Three key areas

This chapter will help you to kick-start your fundraising work. It focuses on three critical areas:

1. Building a vision (pages 23-34)
This will help you to be clear about the specific things you need to raise money for.

2. Appointing a fundraising coordinator (pages 35-43)
Your work will not be effective without this person.

3. Principal funding streams (pages 44-56)
A guide to the types of funding opportunities that await you.

The need for a vision

The best fundraising occurs when the work feeds into a clear overall **vision** of what you want your school to become. THINK BIG! Some of the most outstanding educational opportunities have resulted from being prepared to be really imaginative or ambitious with a vision. Some real examples include:

- The country's first ethical business and enterprise college
- A world-class science centre based on education about tropical orchids
- A primary school with a major football academy on its grounds
- A family community learning centre, with classes during the school day as well as out of hours

Once you are clear about your vision, then you will be able to work out how much money you need to make it a reality. If there is no overall vision for where your school is going, then you will find it hard to target your fundraising work. Or worse, you will just have the vague notion of wanting to get your hands on as much money as possible, for whatever seems like the top priority at that time.

An inclusive vision

In times of old, it would have been the headteacher's role to come up with the vision, and to delegate key tasks to others to bring that vision to reality. These days, management styles have changed for the better, and the best headteachers are those that give leadership by providing the conditions for their staff to find creative solutions themselves.

For example, this could be a special meeting that allows all staff to contribute their ideas to an inspirational session on the future of the school. Sometimes, the headteacher might propose an outline vision that can be discussed and refined in association with the staff. If done sensitively, with quality time given to the process, then the outcome should be that all staff share ownership of the vision and a good proportion will be excited about making things happen. Invest time in these people – they will help you achieve success and will pull the 'anchor draggers' who are resistant to change along with them.

Be prepared to change

'Change is the only constant!
Don't get hung up on the idea
that your vision can't be
altered along the way.
It's having that initial vision
that gets you started on the
road to improvement.'

Building your vision

A meaningful vision is inspirational, realistic and involves not just staff but also the wider community in its formation. Identifying where you want your school to be in three, five or even ten years' time is a powerful way of demonstrating to people (not least your colleagues) that you are striving to improve on the status quo.

But be careful not to go for the safe option which may be highly realistic, yet lacking in imagination. Our studies of outstanding schools have shown that even the most ambitious and far-reaching vision **can** be realised – if you are determined enough to keep at it through the rough and smooth.

You can get good ideas by looking at what other schools have done, but the most appropriate vision for your school depends on **local circumstances** and the skills and creativity of the people who contribute to building your vision. This is why you should involve as many staff as possible in the process.

Sharing the vision

Schools are the focal point of any community. Community members, local businesses, parents and health officials are all affected by what goes on in school. Involve them in this visioning exercise and you may well end up with community champions who will reach those parts others can't reach!

Once you've developed that vision shout it from the roof-tops! Don't just write a letter to parents that might well end up as annoying fluff in the washing machine.

- Inform parents in creative ways that will have impact (see pages 43 & 100)
- Enlist the support of the Local Education Authority, council officials, your MP or MEP, especially if you are developing a really exciting project
- Engage with the local community – they may have picked up along the way that exciting things are starting to happen at your school, so invite groups in or get out to community forum meetings to spread the word. Your community champions will support you if this is new territory

Working with your community

Although many schools have had an active community focus for some time, the government has begun to formalise such work. New specialist schools, for example, must include specific targets around community use of their facilities, and all schools are now expected to forge links locally, organising activities that will benefit as wide a range of people as possible. In many areas **extended schools** are becoming a reality.

The more you can involve the wider community in your work, the more likely you are to be funded. Considering the community when devising new projects should be a routine part of project development at your school.

What can you get money for?

Although there are certainly hundreds of millions of pounds in external funding available to schools, there are some areas which are very difficult to fund.

Generally speaking, you'll find it hard to fund aspects of your school that are concerned with its day-to-day **statutory obligations** to teach the national curriculum. This includes teacher salaries, standard classroom equipment and your school's running costs. Most funders believe government funding should cover all this, and asking for a top-up for general funds is unlikely to result in assistance.

Funders are, however, often interested in projects and key initiatives that add something new to what you offer at the moment. This includes out-of-school-hours provision and work that embraces your community role. It's very helpful to bear this in mind when formulating fundraising plans.

The project-based approach

Throughout this book we frequently mention the value of devising specific **projects** that can be funded, initiatives that:

- Can easily be summarised in a paragraph or a few bullet points
- You can demonstrate a clear need for
- Have educational outcomes or benefits that are far-reaching but realistic
- Can be accurately costed
- Can be carried out according to a meaningful timetable

Schools that are successful at fundraising embrace this approach and are continually devising new projects that fit these criteria.

What scale?

Once you've built your vision you should be able to judge more accurately into which of the following three categories your fundraising work will fall:

1. **Opportunistic fundraising** – amounts of £5,000 or less a year, gained mainly through school events and activities.
2. **Minor campaign fundraising** – amounts of between £5,000 and £45,000 a year, often for specific capital improvements or projects which will require bids to major funders.
3. **Major campaign fundraising** – amounts over £45,000 a year for large-scale projects, such as a new building or matched funding for a specialist school bid.

Having decided this, you will be better able to judge how much effort will be needed to bring in the funds you need.

What scale?

As a rule of thumb, most funding specialists agree that to be successful you need to invest about **10%** of the sum you are seeking in time and resources. The following table indicates the likely effort needed to succeed in fundraising at the three levels.

Type of fundraising	Time commitment	Other considerations
Opportunistic (up to £5,000 a year)	Whatever is available on an ad hoc basis.	This can sometimes be done by the PTA alone, with little staff involvement.
Minor campaign (£5,000-£45,000 a year)	At least one hour per week, rising to two or three hours per week for larger sums.	Regular meetings (at least once a half-term) should take place between the fundraising coordinator and headteacher.
Major campaign (over £45,000 a year)	At least a day a week, or equivalent; the more money needed the larger the time commitment. For sums over £1,000,000 a full-time coordinator (or external consultant) would normally be required.	A small fundraising team, including a member of SMT and a governor, should be formed to guide the overall campaign.

How much?

This book is aimed mainly at schools that wish to engage in minor or major campaign fundraising. If you're happy with opportunistic fundraising you're likely to be already achieving the sums you're after, which are easy to raise through school events.

How much money you can attract to your school depends on the following factors:

- The skills and experience of the fundraising coordinator
- The support of others in the school and community – this needs to be cultivated
- The time dedicated to the role
- A certain amount of luck – but remember you largely create your own! (It's true – see Wiseman 2003 for details)
- The extent to which effective partnerships with others can be built

It's not just about money!

Money makes the world go round, but other things can keep it spinning! Although much of this book will focus on strategies to get your hands on grants or cash for your school, you can also make your school budgets go further in other ways, eg:

- Accepting donations of equipment or materials, or taking advantage of the various schemes for refurbished or second-hand items. A company may not be able to help with cash but may have huge stock-piles of items that you could utilise, for cut-price or even free
- Using professional assistance and volunteer time creatively. Through networking and sharing the vision, you will undoubtedly meet people who want to help which may not bring you money but will save you from spending it!

Remember, if you can attach a monetary value to these donations you may well be able to match fund against them (page 56). Do not forget too that saving energy, telephone and water costs can help to improve overall funding for your school. (See pages 54-55).

Appointing a fundraising coordinator

One of the biggest mistakes you can make is to think you can raise the money you need in the scraps of time left over at the end of the week. If your school is serious about fundraising, then it must have a **fundraising coordinator**. This does NOT have to be a full-time appointment – half a day, or a couple of hours a week, is a good start. This person can

- Take an overview of all fundraising activities at your school
- Be a first point of contact within and outside the organisation
- Make sure that your school in on track to meet its targets

Our studies of schools that are successful at fundraising convince us that, financially, it is always worth appointing somebody to oversee fundraising. Schools that have done so have brought in enough funds to cover salary and training costs many times over and have generated substantial income for whole school developments that would simply not have been otherwise possible.

What should the role encompass?

The fundraising coordinator should have a **job description** that outlines duties, eg:

- Carrying out fundraising audits
- Preparing and revising fundraising development plans
- Liaising with governors, senior management and other staff on fundraising issues
- Identifying funding sources
- Keeping up to date with rules governing bids
- Preparing project proposals and bids
- Meeting potential sponsors
- Coordinating whole-school fundraising events and activities
- Monitoring and evaluating projects

The need for delegation

There is only one hard and fast rule about who should take on the role of coordinating fundraising: it should **not** be the headteacher. The head should be actively involved in supporting the coordinator, but we believe this is a role that should be **delegated**, even in small primary schools.

The **personal qualities** to look for in a fundraising coordinator include:

- Imagination
- Determination
- An ability to juggle deadlines
- Meticulous organisation
- Confidence in meeting people
- Good writing skills

The right person for the job

As the following examples from real schools illustrate, the person with the qualities to bring you fundraising success may come from any of several areas within a school:

- A **deputy headteacher** with a business background who wishes to take on the role as part of her wider responsibility for community relations
- A **business manager** who carries out fundraising duties alongside his other financial functions
- A **head of department** with a flair for fundraising who is happy to take on this additional whole-school responsibility in return for additional pay
- A part-time member of **admin** staff with experience of the business world who is employed solely to coordinate fundraising

Consider looking **outside** your school too. Some schools have found excellent part-time fundraisers by advertising in the local or regional newspaper.

Supporting the postholder

Anybody who takes on the fundraising brief must receive adequate support in their role. There is a key balance to be struck between support at a strategic and managerial level and support of an administrative nature.

Administrative

- Writing initial letters
- Routine telephone calls
- Chasing up appointments
- Keeping abreast of the latest funding streams

Strategic and managerial

- Whole school issues
- Strategic input to fundraising plans
- Links to the school development/improvement plan
- Specialist input to bids

Supporting the postholder

The balance of support will depend on a number of factors, including the coordinator's previous experience and skills, their other responsibilities and the amount of time they have to carry out the role.

A deputy head
'I will be able to carry out most strategic tasks, but will need to be supported with administrative duties, otherwise I will soon become overwhelmed by these. I need an admin mentor!'

A member of admin staff
'I am happy to perform administrative tasks and a few strategic duties, but will need specialist input on plans and bids from a more senior member of staff and would appreciate support in high-level meetings with funders. I need a management mentor!'

Other support mechanisms

The more people that support the fundraising coordinator, the better his or her work will be. This could include:

- Administrative or strategic support as appropriate
- Regular meetings with the headteacher and governors to discuss progress
- Day-to-day moral support from the headteacher and governors
- Support from other staff, such as subject leaders, including specialist input to bids and notice of new funding priorities or opportunities in their subject areas

Some schools manage to set up small **support teams** for their fundraising coordinator, comprising a member of the senior management team, a governor, a member of the parent-teacher association and a community representative. Such people can provide valuable guidance, may help out with organisational or administrative tasks, or may be on hand to help at school events.

Internal communication

One of the key aspects of the fundraising coordinator's role is effective **communication** with staff on fundraising issues. Communication can be improved by:

- **Issuing a termly or half-termly news sheet** (one side of A4 would be fine) – this should update staff on fundraising news and successes, invite ideas, or appeal for individuals to help with specific projects
- **Having a regular five-minute slot in staff meetings** – this could cover similar ground to the news sheet, but could also provide staff with the opportunity to ask questions. It will help keep fundraising high on everyone's agenda
- **Meeting key staff on a regular basis** – in addition to the head and governors this may include subject leaders, or other staff coordinating whole school issues. Make sure that all such meetings are booked in diaries in advance

External communication

It's vital to take every opportunity to let the **wider community** know about your work. Success breeds success, and you will sometimes find that simply by publicising your work others are drawn to offer their support.

Effective external communication can be achieved through:

- A school magazine or newsletter
- Regular press releases to local papers
- Displays in libraries, local supermarkets and other public places
- Mentioning fundraising work at public events such as open or parents' evenings (see page 100)

If your school has a press officer, they should support this communication work. They may, for example, already have good media contacts that will help secure such things as local radio interviews. For further guidance on effective communication see *Promoting Your School Pocketbook* (2006)

Overview of funding streams

It's beyond the scope of this book to include a complete breakdown of the external funding sources available to schools. There are many thousands of potential sources, with new ones being launched all the time.

Instead, what we provide is an overview of the main types of funding, with details of where to go to find out more. There are also some excellent books and electronic databases to help you to begin the process of finding specific funders for your projects (details on pages 122-125).

Main funding sources

The main **funding sources** for schools are:

- Non-statutory government grants (eg specialist schools initiative. See www.standards.dfes.gov.uk for other schemes)
- The National Lottery
- Grant-making trusts
- Awards and competitions
- European funding
- Business donations
- School appeals and events
- Income generation from the school buildings/grounds

The National Lottery

Since its beginning in 1994 the National Lottery has handed out tens of billions of pounds to good causes. Schools are welcome to make applications for **all** lottery grants, providing certain conditions are met.

There are five lottery distributors relevant to schools:

- The **Arts Council** (www.artscouncil.org.uk)
- The **Heritage Lottery Fund** (www.hlf.org.uk)
- The **Big Lottery Fund** (www.biglotteryfund.org.uk) – formed in 2004 from the merger of the New Opportunities Fund and the Community Fund
- The **Sports Councils** (e.g. www.sportengland.org)
- The **National Foundation for Youth Music** (www.youthmusic.org.uk)

The highly popular **Awards for All** (www.awardsforall.org.uk) scheme is joint-funded by all four of the above bodies. It provides grants of up to £5,000 to schools, with a sizeable number of schools having benefited so far.

Grant-making trusts

These are usually set up by wealthy individuals or companies and many schools have successfully applied for funds. Most trusts only accept applications from registered charities, so it's worth getting charitable status for your school or PTA/friends group (see page 114 for details).

Top tips:

- Do as much research as you can before starting to apply to a specific trust

- Target your applications carefully – go for a maximum of three trusts for each project (see page 123 for details of databases to search)

- Draw attention to the uniqueness of your project – what will make it stand out from the crowd and how will it be innovative?

- Very few trusts are interested in making general donations to schools, but many will consider a project that gives young people new educational opportunities

Grant-making trusts

Top tips:

- Trusts are often specific in the type of activity they will support – there is no point trying to bend your application to make it fit the criteria

- Many trusts give grants to just one (sometimes small) geographical area – it's important to check this before making an application

- Most trusts require you to write a letter of application; some require you to complete their own application form

- Applying to trusts can be time-consuming and some trusts are inundated with applications, so do not expect to be successful every time you apply, and keep the number of applications to a manageable size

European funding

Most large-scale funds from Europe are channelled through your LEA for specific projects, often around regeneration. If you are after these types of funds you should liaise with your LEA European funding officer who will have more details of the funds available in your area.

Some of the vast finances of the EU can be harnessed by your school if you wish to gain funds to develop the European dimension through curriculum work and exchanges. There are generous grants available to support schools' work in these areas, particularly through the Comenius Programme. (See www.socrates-uk.net for advice and example projects).

Many of the current schemes are so far rather undersubscribed and excellent support is available from the International Resource Centre for Schools and Colleges at the University of Hull (contact details on page 125).

Business donations

As well as working with local businesses, you may be able to tap into the resources of larger, national companies.

Top tips:

- Keep a lookout for schemes run by companies in the press
- Eastwood *et al.* (2001) contains a very useful section on the charitable activities of major business in the UK
- Bear in mind what's in it for the business
- Be prepared to court local business through events and networking

Awards and competitions

Thumbing through any issue of the *Times Educational Supplement*, you will be hard-pressed not to find at least one competition aimed at schools. Many of these have substantial cash prizes, or items of equipment that any school would welcome. However, competitions also offer the opportunity for a range of stimulating project work, both within and outside the national curriculum. Sometimes, though, it's possible just to submit students' work which has been prepared as part of normal lessons. Many schemes are undersubscribed so give them a go!

Top tips:

- You've got to be in to win! Look out for details of competitions in the press and get into the habit of submitting entries
- Read the judging criteria carefully and make sure your entry fits these
- Look at winning entries to give you an idea of what judges are looking for
- Give yourself plenty of time to meet the deadline so the entry isn't rushed
- Even if you don't win, make the most of your participation, with articles in the school newsletter and local press, and display students' entries prominently in school

School appeals and events

There are many ways in which schools can raise funds from the community through specific appeals or events, ranging from fashion parades to cookery demonstrations. These can often be linked to school projects or examination work, and getting students to help organise such events is an excellent way for them to gain invaluable life skills. It also gives them a role in shaping their school's future.

Imagination and creativity are often the keys to success. The advantage of this type of fundraising is that the timing is flexible and cash raised can be channelled directly to your priority areas, rather than being tied into a specific project or bid. Don't neglect the potential of well-organised and well-publicised fêtes and fairs to raise income on a one-off basis. Auctions of promises seem to have been particularly successful in recent years in a variety of schools.

Your students themselves are often a superb source of ideas for these kinds of fundraising events, and getting the whole school involved can be a great way of bringing staff and students closer together.

Income generation from buildings/grounds

Your school buildings and grounds represent a major, but often under-utilised, resource that can bring in additional funds. To harness such funds a change in attitude may be required by your school to behave more like a business. It will also help if you can develop imaginative ideas for raising funds using your buildings and grounds. (See page 117.)

To be successful with this type of fundraising, a considerable amount of marketing, which should be overseen by the school fundraising coordinator, will be required. It will also be necessary to liaise with the LEA on the suitability of your proposals regarding health and safety.

Some enterprising schools have entered the education software world by designing products that help teachers use ICT in the classroom. These have brought in significant additional funds to the schools concerned.   One example is Dixons City Technology College, Bradford, which has raised substantial funds through a highly innovative business studies package (see page 125 for contact details). But this is a major undertaking and may be out of reach for many schools.

Other ways to make or save money

When it comes to energy use, schools typically **waste** thousands of pounds a year and send all the wrong environmental messages in doing so. Simple measures (such as energy-efficient light bulbs and movement-sensitive light switches) can often make a big difference. There is also a range of companies and charities that will convert your used printer and photocopier cartridges into cash.

Get help to go green!
Contact your Local Education Authority or CREATE (www.create.org.uk) and consider your institution's fuel bills and environmental policy. Energy audits help to instigate change and identify areas for improvement.

Making the most of your resources

We're so pressured to make the budget balance that often we don't think beyond one financial year. Installing thermostatic radiator valves, intelligent lighting controls and secondary glazing in one year will dent the finances, but bite the bullet as one year's outlay will be rewarded by reduced costs year-on-year. Think too about working together with your school clusters or within your family of schools. Do you purchase everything separately? Bulk buying may attract savings.

When you've attracted funds or so called 'clean money' do you explore matched funding against this? You may be able to double the amount (see next page).

The greatest resource you have is the people around you. Are they encouraged to pursue fundraising avenues or is it just *your* job? Unlock their potential, listen to their ideas; they may have a refreshing approach!

Matched funding

An entire book could be devoted to the subject of **matched** (or match) funding! Don't be fazed by the strange world that is matched funding. It essentially means finding additional money or resources for a project from sources outside the main grant. Some funding sources (eg, the specialist schools scheme and some of the National Lottery grants) contain a **compulsory** element of matched funding. This means that you will only get the grant if you can find the extra funds yourself. Other funding bodies give you some of the money you need and leave you to find the rest yourself.

This is a classic situation where you should not be afraid to ask for help. Unless you have an abundance of time and an inquisitive nature, it's best to contact the person in your LEA with responsibility for this area, or to seek further guidance from the specific funder. Our experiences of working with LEA officers have been very favourable, and significant matched funding *can* be secured.

People don't always realise that offers of labour can count as matched funding. There are standard hourly rates applicable for different kinds of work.

Setting
the Scene

 Getting
Started

 The Ten-Step
Model

 Fundraising
in Action

 Monitoring
and
Evaluating

 Tools/Further
Information

The Ten-Step Model

An overall strategy for success

A fundraising strategy is the **big picture** that outlines how you will go about getting the funds you need. It includes:

- A vision of where the work is taking you
- The ethics and protocols that underpin your work
- The systems you'll set up to get the work going and keep it on track
- The people who'll be involved, how much time they'll spend, and their roles and responsibilities
- A detailed development plan which shows the actions that will be carried out over a two-to-three-year timescale
- Specific projects for which you're chasing funds within an agreed timescale
- How the work will dovetail with other key aspects of the school's plans
- How your work will be monitored and evaluated, including judging its success

The step-by-step model that follows will only be fully effective if it operates within the framework of such an overall strategy for success.

A strategic approach

If you don't have a well-thought-out **strategy**, then you are not likely to raise the money you need in the timescale you've set out. Either it will take you two or three times as long – or worse still, you will never attain your fundraising targets.

Following a strategic approach, such as the one outlined in this book, will make your work cost-effective in terms of time and resources. It will also give you a point of reference to go back to if you feel you need to refine your approach or assess particular aspects of your work.

It's easy to become frustrated with fundraising work, with so many balls to juggle, deadlines to meet and leads to chase. On top of that you have to deal with rejected bids, even though you felt you met the criteria. No one is 100% successful in their applications. Having a strategy which underpins your work can give you the confidence to keep going, knowing that your school has put a lot of thought into the approach you are following. Such thinking and planning time is never wasted.

Step-by-step

The following step-by-step model will help you optimise your fundraising work. Its key underpinning principle is that you have an overall **vision** for your school and where you are heading (see pages 23-34).

1 Appoint somebody to coordinate the fundraising work.
2 Audit existing fundraising practice.
3 Establish your school's current development priorities.
4 Identify which school priorities need additional funding.
5 Establish how much money is needed and over what timescale.
6 Write a fundraising development plan for the next two to three years.
7 Prepare summary proposals for each individual project.
8 Match the funds required for each project to the most appropriate sources.
9 Review your fundraising efforts at regular intervals.
10 Celebrate success!

Ethics and principles

It's important to agree some fundamental **ethics** and **principles** that inform your fundraising work and reflect the values of your school. Your school vision will be the product of many hours of consultation and deliberation. This could all be compromised by ill-chosen schemes, or accepting the first offer of money that comes your way. Don't be tempted into an association that will tarnish your reputation.

Ethics and principles

- Be prepared to refuse offers of money if a source is considered inappropriate, sure in the knowledge that better, 'cleaner' offers will be around the corner
- Consider how far you are prepared to go – would you want to be re-named a 'McFry's Community School'?
- Be clear about such issues as whether or not you want to promote the collection of tokens from unhealthy drinks and foods
- Agree what is acceptable and not acceptable practice in working with parents/carers. (Do you want to encourage gambling, for example?)

If your vision is bold enough and successes have been achieved, more people will want to be associated with you. Be patient and don't sell your soul to the devil in the name of progress.

Step 1: Appoint a fundraising coordinator

See pages 35-43 of the Getting Started section for
a detailed look at the role of the fundraising
coordinator and at the importance of
appointing someone to this position as a
first step.

Step 2: Audit existing practice

Before you begin any new fundraising work at your school, it's critical to take stock of the current situation. This is done most effectively through a **fundraising audit** that:

1. Records key information about work done to date, providing a baseline from which you can judge future progress.
2. Brings together information that may otherwise be scattered in various places.

Include in your audit:

*   How fundraising is currently organised
*   Fundraising successes to date, with details of source, date gained, methods used, etc
*   Sources used to find out about funding opportunities
*   Details of any existing fundraising targets
*   Progress with any fundraising development plans already in place

You may find the audit template opposite helpful.

Step 2: Audit existing practice

Audit template

1. Date; name of person completing audit.
2. Is there a named person responsible for fundraising at your school? If so, who and what is their job title/role?
3. Does anybody at your school have any dedicated time to carry out this role? If it's a paid member of staff, quantify how much time they spend on fundraising activities each week.
4. Are there formal meetings with senior management/governors to discuss fundraising specifically? How often?
5. Who else is actively involved in fundraising for your school? Explain what they have done and how it has helped. This could include staff or other people.
6. List any successful examples of fundraising by your school in the last two years. (Give details in a table of month/year, amount raised, how you raised it, what the money was used for.)
7. What sources of information have been used to identify funding opportunities?
8. What are your school's current fundraising targets? List as many as possible, but in priority order.
9. Do you have a fundraising development plan? Describe what it contains.

Step 2: Audit existing practice

You should carry out a new fundraising audit at least once a year, so that **progress** can be judged. It will also serve as a means of monitoring and evaluating your work.

As you begin to make fresh fundraising plans, it's important you have background information to hand. If you've not already done this, the audit gives you the chance to bring all the important documents together in one place – letters of application, completed bids, newspaper clippings etc. These should be placed in a well-labelled filing system so you can find things again quickly.

Over the course of a year your fundraising files should grow in size considerably, so time spent setting up a rigorous system at the start is really worthwhile.

Step 3: Establish school development priorities

Your school will probably have identified a number of **priorities** for development over the coming few years. These will be included in the whole school **development plan** (or school improvement plan) and refer to innovations or projects which the school has committed to undertake to address specific issues.

Once your school has committed to a fundraising drive it seems sensible to consider these priority areas first. As your time is limited, focus your effort on those areas considered most fundamental to the future of the school. Of course, your visioning exercise may have identified exciting new ideas not built into the official development plan that need to be considered too. Now may be the time to revise your school development plan to take account of any new direction for your school.

You also need to have a clear idea of the **priority order** in which issues are to be tackled. Make a list of what the published priorities are and consider how any new ones fit in, in rank order. Better still, arrange to see the headteacher to have a detailed discussion about your school development plan: it should become a familiar friend in the years to come.

Step 4: Which priorities need additional funding?

Having identified the main development priorities for your school, be clear which of these need **additional funding**? This might sound like a silly question to those who don't have to write school development plans, but it does need some careful thought.

The school development plan sets out the actions that will be taken in order to meet particular targets agreed between the headteacher and governors. Some, perhaps even all, of these may concern areas that will already be **funded through statutory routes** (eg, Excellence in Cities, Standards Fund, LEA buildings fund, etc). You need to discover if there are priorities identified in the school development plan that require **external funding**, or would benefit from it. Make a note of such priorities under these two headings.

If your school is new to fundraising, then your senior management team may not be used to identifying priorities in the school development plan that require *additional* funding. But your vision exercise may have conjured up a range of new initiatives for which you do not currently have the money.

Step 5: How much is needed and by when?

The purpose of this exercise is to set some fundraising **targets** for which you can set a realistic timescale. Beginning with the top priority for your school, determine how much it will cost as precisely as you can. This is vital as you need to have the figures before you can decide how much time you will need to spend trying to get the money. If your top priority is a major project, then it's likely that this will be the **only** priority you will tackle at the moment. Don't try to be overambitious by taking on too much at once.

Examples of fundraising targets include:
* £25,000 to update a science laboratory, needed by September 2006
* £10,000 for a project focusing on underachievement of a specific group of children, needed by Easter 2006
* £3,000 to set up an after school maths club, needed by the end of autumn term 2006
* £8,000 for a literacy summer school, needed by the start of summer holiday 2006

Step 6: Write fundraising development plan

Once you've identified fundraising targets you can begin to carry out the actions that will enable you to reach them in an appropriate timescale. This is where your **fundraising development plan** is essential.

Development plans are now a familiar feature of school management. They set out key information about the tasks that need to be carried out to meet targets, usually **over a two-to-three-year timescale**. They're most useful when laid out in tabular form and should include as headings:

- **Target** – be clear about what you are aiming to do
- **Action** – be as precise as you can here about the steps needed
- **Responsibility** – who's going to do it? Do others have a role?
- **Cost** – every action brings a cost of one sort or another
- **Timing** – when will it be done?
- **Monitoring and evaluation** – how will you monitor progress and judge success?

Every two to three years rewrite your plan to take account of new priorities.

Step 7: Prepare summary proposals for each project

For every project you've devised it's important to be able to describe in a nutshell what you want to achieve. This is where your **summary proposal** comes in. (You might find the template on page 115 a useful starting point.) If you prepare it electronically, it will be a very helpful document you can use in a variety of ways to take the project forward, not least when making funding applications.

A summary proposal is a 500-word description of your project including:
- Its aims
- Why it's needed and how that need has been identified
- The benefits or outcomes it will bring
- How it will make a difference to your students and the wider community
- The budget needed
- Timescales
- Roles and responsibilities
- Monitoring and evaluation procedures

Step 8: Match funds required to most appropriate sources

Your fundraising development plan will indicate the need to raise a specific sum of money for a major project, or smaller sums for a number of minor projects. But how do you narrow down the search for funders from many thousands of potential sources?

A lot of time can be wasted if you are not realistic about matching your needs very precisely to the criteria of the funders. It's vital to match the funds you require to the most appropriate sources.

Step 8: Match funds required to most appropriate sources

Strategies to find appropriate funders for your projects:

- **Research** the funders well, using books, newspapers and newsletters, the internet and electronic databases to home-in on the most appropriate sources (see pages 122-124). Don't forget the flyers that routinely come into your school, many of which are, in turn, routinely recycled!

- **Discuss** your proposals with the funders if they will allow this. Many funders are now very approachable and this will save you a lot of time

- **Be realistic** about where to go to get the funds you need – for example, if you are seeking a large sum for a new build project, then trying to raise it through parental contributions and school fairs is simply not sensible

If you are making formal written bids to specific funders, make sure you target no more than **three** at one time and prepare very careful applications. Otherwise, you will end up doing a huge amount of speculative work, and could easily get frustrated.

Step 9: Review regularly

It's critical to **review** how your fundraising work is progressing from time to time. This will help you judge whether you are on track to reach your target(s), and indicate if alternative strategies need to be used.

Reviewing your work in this way is a key **monitoring** technique. It can be easy to neglect during your busy working week, so record in your diary when it will be done and make sure you set aside the time to do it.

Monitoring also includes considering individual projects and making sure things are progressing to schedule. You should also make sure that all your projects are **evaluated** to determine whether they had the intended impact. Further guidance in this area is given on pages 104-112.

Step 10: Celebrate success!

Make time to **mark your successes**, however small they may seem. Fundraising can be really hard work and it's important to recognise when your efforts have borne fruit. Involve pupils in the celebrations and remember, success breeds success. Marking your achievements not only boosts your confidence, it also shows potential funders that good things are happening in your school.

You can celebrate success in a number of ways, including:

- Staging a public celebration for a major success. Plan it well in advance

- Issuing press releases to local media and inviting key personnel from your local newspapers to any events

- Setting up displays or a celebration board

- Telling others about it

- Photographing the proceedings – you can show the images to potential funders

- Having a little celebration yourself with family and friends

Innovation and ambition

Remember in all your fundraising work the need to be **creative** and **bold**! For example, schools spend thousands of pounds each year on their energy needs. If you asked a potential supporter to foot the bill for your electricity supply you can guess the outcome. If, however, you approached them with the proposal to install a solar water-heating unit that would:

- Reduce your energy bills
- Provide a teaching tool for both science and design technology
- Send a very strong environmental message that could be drawn upon in citizenship

Then the outcome may be very different.

Keep in mind also that many funders want to be associated with large projects that are likely to make a significant impact. Do some 'blue-sky thinking' during that visioning session (page 24) to devise some really meaningful projects.

Setting
the Scene

 Getting
Started

 The Ten-Step
Model

 Fundraising
in Action

 Monitoring
and
Evaluating

 Tools/Further
Information

Fundraising in Action

Bids

One of the main tasks for a school fundraising coordinator is the submission of **completed bids** to funders. These are usually several pages long, and sometimes must be filled in on the funders' application forms. Completing your first bid can seem daunting, but with practice you *will* get better and quicker at the process. Remember, it's a specific skill to learn.

It's sometimes helpful to view it in the same light as a job application. You will need to use positive language, talk your project up and make it stand out from the crowd. Treat it as carefully as you would a job application – provide all the information that is requested and do not miss any sections out.

Bid writing is a lengthy process. If you are finding it quick and easy then you are probably not doing your bids justice!

Successful bid writing

Use the following sequence for successful bid writing and see the next page for examples of the kind of positive, persuasive language to use in your submissions.

- Discuss your project idea with key people in your area – this could include the LEA, neighbouring schools, other partners
- Write a summary proposal on computer first (see page 71)
- Narrow down your search to about ten potential funders and get their application packs – these are your 'longlist'
- Scrutinise their criteria further to create a 'shortlist' of no more than three funders that look extremely promising
- If possible, discuss your project with funders
- Draft out your bid, using your summary proposal as a guide
- Seek specialist input from other staff where necessary
- Have someone else read over the bid for clarity
- Let the bid 'mature' for a few days before re-reading it and sending it off
- Make sure you keep a copy of the bid for future reference

Examples from successful bids

We are launching this project because a community consultation exercise has highlighted the need for...

Our students, through their student council, have made it clear that a priority area for disaffected boys is...

This work will make a lasting impact on our school due to its...

The aims of the project embrace school and community needs and include...

We will achieve these aims through a range of innovative approaches, such as...

Our collaboration with two local schools will enhance the impact of this project and ensure a wider range of people will benefit from it...

The target groups for this initiative have been identified by...

A key element in this project will be partnership, which will be achieved by...

This work builds on already well-established practice that needs to be extended if its influence is to be felt by a wider student cohort...

We will be monitoring and evaluating the project using a range of qualitative and quantitative data, including...

In order to ensure continuity and sustainability we will...

Completing application forms

Before sending off your application form, ask yourself the following questions:

- Have you completed all the sections you need to in full?
- Have you included everything requested in the application pack?
- Have you included extra enclosures only if they're permitted?
- Have you made clear the benefits of your project to your students and the wider community?
- Does the budget make sense and is it realistic?
- Have you avoided using education jargon?

Some schools have had their applications refused for simple, administrative reasons. Don't get caught out like this.

The project manager

When developing projects it's vital to have identified a **project manager**, someone to lead the project if the application is successful. In many cases this person will *not* be the fundraising coordinator. (Their principal role should be to obtain funds and coordinate fundraising.) Equally, one person cannot possibly be project manager for all the school's projects.

The definition of project manager here is quite broad and could include:

- A teacher who manages the setting up of a new dance club
- A deputy headteacher who manages the updating of the science labs
- The head of PE who manages the upgrading of the school's sports equipment
- A member of the PTA who volunteers to coordinate an event or activity

The project manager

Tasks that typically will be carried out by the project manager include:

- Explaining the project to other people involved, eg students, staff and parents/carers
- Taking day-to-day responsibility for the project, eg chairing meetings, getting supplies ordered, making bookings etc.
- Organising staff and liaising with outside agencies
- Making sure everything is progressing on time
- Writing, or contributing to the writing of, project reports or evaluations

The project manager may benefit from some administrative support in carrying out some of these tasks. Funding for this can often be included in bids.

The project manager

In some cases a project may be so large and complicated (eg a new building) that a **professional project manager** is brought in as part of the contract. In these cases a senior member of staff should be appointed to liaise with the professional.

Smaller scale, but still significant projects (eg a major curriculum innovation) sometimes benefit from the appointment of a staff **project management team** rather than an individual project manager. Here, the individuals within the team can be assigned key tasks so that everyone knows what their roles and responsibilities are, but there should still be a single person who takes overall charge.

Spread the load

If you've set about realising a bold vision for your school, you won't achieve it on your **own**. Think creatively about the people around you and how they might be best able to help.

Who can help?

- Teaching staff
- Retired teaching staff
- Supply teaching staff
- Non-teaching staff
- Community champions
- PTA activists
- Students
- Former students
- Parents
- Council officers, MPs, MEPs

Spread the load

Teaching staff
You will know who to engage from your staff and what strategies you need to employ to get their involvement. Staff can be very powerful advocates for the school's work in the community, so do use them to help spread the message.

Retired teaching staff
Some retired staff may never wish to raise a pen again, but for others, severing the ties they have with their school may be very difficult. They may welcome the opportunity of helping with the search for funding. For example, they could:

*   Scan **newspapers** for funding opportunities – local papers will often carry adverts from companies keen to boost their community profile. Daily papers and the TES may publicise national competitions that schools or community groups can apply for

*   Identify suitable **charitable trusts** from sources in the local library

Spread the load

Supply teaching staff

Many schools have a loyal band of regular supply staff, some of whom may have a real connection or affinity with the school and may well offer services beyond the normal work of a supply teacher. You will know if this is a possibility at your school.

Non-teaching staff

This key group of workers is often overlooked. Spending time with non-teaching staff will pay dividends in many respects. Many of these staff will live in the heart of the community your school serves. Like it or not, they will influence how others see the school. Their views will be sought by local people in shops, clubs and pubs, and if they're disenfranchised, negative views will spread. If they buy into the vision, however, the opposite will happen and they may well become your community champions.

Spread the load

Community champions
Pillars of the local area with networks to dream of, these people can help you raise thousands of pounds. If they can't do it themselves, then they know someone who can. Court them fiercely as they can make a huge difference. They could include business people, church figures, charity leaders, politicians or campaigners. Consider how to access these people and invite them into school.

PTA activists
These may well be your community champions given a posh title! They may also include governors with a wealth of experience and contacts. Many PTAs are now gaining charitable status and this opens doors to a whole raft of funding that schools couldn't otherwise access (see page 114). One PTA in a Stockport school has raised £147,000 in the last few years!

Students
Don't **underestimate** how much a group of motivated students can do with the right direction, encouragement and success (see pages 101-102).

Spread the load

Former students
The advent of Friends Reunited has allowed huge numbers of former students to re-engage with their old school. Court these people. Give them a spot on your school website and invite them into school for reunions. Make the most of such occasions and present your vision (early in the evening – these events tend to be boozy affairs!). You may be surprised where some of your students have ended up and they may well buy into your vision.

Parents/carers
Some headteachers are nervous about fully involving their parents and carers in the fundraising scene. It never fails to amaze us how little information gets home via their children. Parents and carers can make a **huge** difference to your fundraising.

Council officers
Many local councils have officers tasked with finding 'funny money!' These people may have expertise with lottery funding or the intricacies of European funding and can steer you through the morass of matched funding.

Network!

Go looking for contacts with confidence,
enthusiasm and determination.

Finding businesses to work with

Local businesses can be an excellent source of additional support for your school. Gathering information about potential local business sponsors is an important process. Sources of information include:

- Yellow Pages
- Your students and their parents/carers
- Ex-students
- Staff
- Governors
- The local Chamber of Trade

You are much more likely to receive support from a company if they have some sort of **link** to your school, eg an ex-student, parents/carers who work there.

Creating business links

Many businesses donate cash or resources to schools as part of their community work, or in return for positive publicity. **Cultivating strong links** with the managers of key local businesses can reap far-reaching benefits for your school.

Some schools are also discovering the value of involving such companies in delivering **curriculum programmes**, as the benefits students can derive from working with local employers can be considerable.

Businesses are usually keen to provide support for a **specific** initiative (eg, equipping an ICT room, providing new playground equipment), rather than providing general donations. An example letter for use with local companies appears on the next page.

Example letter to business

Business Address

School address

Dear Mr/Mrs/Ms X

EXCITING OPPORTUNITY AT ANYTOWN SCHOOL

Following our recent community consultation sessions, Anytown School is now embarking on the next phase of its mission to improve education opportunities in the Anytown area. I am writing to invite your company to play its part in helping us achieve our vision.

There are a number of specific projects that I think your company would be attracted to, and we are holding an informal evening session for local businesses on 12 June at 7:00 pm. There will be drinks and light snacks and you will have the opportunity to meet key staff and other businesses who hope to work with us.

Please confirm your attendance at this event by returning the reply slip at the bottom of this letter. If you are unable to attend on this date, I would be delighted to meet you at your business premises to discuss the opportunities we can offer you.

Yours sincerely

Name

Headteacher, Anytown School

Engaging with businesses

In making approaches to businesses, it pays dividends for the **headteacher** to be involved. Seek a contact at the highest level possible in the company and arrange to outline your plans in a meeting which ideally includes the headteacher and a governor. In this way the company will take your approach more seriously, and the donation could be correspondingly greater. Writing stock letters to hundreds of companies is probably the least effective strategy!

When working with businesses it's important to consider what's in it for them. There are often major gains to a company from being associated with a school, eg:

- Positive publicity
- Access to facilities and resources
- Making contacts with future employees
- The feeling of giving something back to the community
- Market research

The art of sponsorship meetings

When you get your opportunity to speak to somebody senior in an organisation make the most of the opportunity. Don't be shy or apologetic – be bold and enthusiastic!

- Prepare thoroughly as you will only get one chance
- Be clear how much time you have
- Be succinct and never under-estimate the power of photographs to convey messages – many business leaders have not been in school for years and a few images of how things are now can speak louder than words
- Be clear about what you want and articulate this
- Stress the reciprocal nature of the relationship and detail what you can offer in return – this could range from access to sporting facilities, IT, reprographics and language expertise, through to prize-giving opportunities

Publicity and support

Make the most of any publicity opportunities offered by business donations and offer to advertise the company's support in your school newsletter or on your website. If you are able to display the company's name prominently in your school this usually helps, and is especially appropriate if they have sponsored a new classroom or facility.

Remember that business may also be able to provide support **in kind** rather than cash. This can still be very valuable, eg:

- Items of equipment you can put to good use
- Goods for school raffles
- Help staging an event
- Marketing expertise
- Health and safety advice
- Personnel to join your governing body

Consider all types of support that businesses can offer you.

Developing your own 'business sense'

Although it demands a special approach, you should soon develop your own sense of how to engage with business. It certainly requires an ability to manage communication and present a positive image effectively.

Some schools are now very outgoing in working with business, organising working breakfasts and cocktail receptions to inform local business leaders of their plans and invite partners to join the school. These schools generally have very strong links with business, many of whom have invested heavily in the school to the benefit of students.

Working with the press

Fundraising successes are always newsworthy, so you should make the most of any publicity opportunities associated with your projects, working in close cooperation with your school press officer, if you have one.

- Issue press releases, which include your full contact details, directly to journalists
- Phone the local papers to let them know about major developments
- Organise photo opportunities involving students
- Place news items in your school newsletter/website

Try to work with a named colleague on each newspaper and invite that person into school. Local newspapers in particular often find it difficult to fill their pages with interesting stories each week, so it's well worth alerting the editors to positive developments at your school.

The press are often accused of distorting the facts, but on many occasions they have not been given them accurately. Having just one person responsible for press liaison reduces the chance of mixed messages and of appearing unprofessional.

Photographs

To maximise the **impact** of photographs, keep those in the picture down to four. If large numbers are important, include them in the background with the main image focusing on a small number in the foreground (large numbers of children lose impact).

Be fiercely critical of **appearance**: ties, make-up, jewellery etc, as image is everything. Provide the picture yourself if a photographer is unavailable and include the names and ages of the students involved. Though it may seem like you're doing all the work here, it's time well spent.

Try to get your **contact details** on the bottom of any photograph or newspaper article. A direct dial telephone number, web or email address will often lead to contact.

Maximising parental interfaces

Your school's **public events** such as parents' and open evenings are fantastic opportunities, not just to show your school off at its best but also to woo parental support.

These occasions also provide access to all walks of life and business.

- Do parents feel welcome and leave feeling they know where the school is going? (This is particularly important to the parents of children just entering the school)
- What might the school be like when their children are taking their final exams?
- They are the stakeholders – provide them not only with the opportunity to engage, but with a chance to contribute to the vision

Amazing parental involvement is possible, even in the toughest of schools, but you need to really work at it. A ten-minute upbeat, inspirational presentation may capture imaginations. Get a buzz going and try to establish links. Have flyers prepared and have a member of staff free for sponsorship referrals.

Involving students

Involving students in raising funds is both practical and **educational**. Students develop numeracy and financial literacy and feel genuinely empowered.

Equally, spelling out in pounds and pence the costs of vandalism, repairs and maintenance, litter collection and electricity bills just may challenge some practices. Fifty pounds replacing a kicked-out window is fifty pounds not spent on new sports equipment. Equating a broken window to a new set of badminton racquets may just bring the school budget into clearer focus.

Involving students

The non-uniform day and the sponsored this-and-that all have their place, but to overdo these things hits the same pockets each time.

- Spending weekends bag-packing at the end of supermarket checkouts can be a worthwhile use of student power, provided the youngsters have a direct vested interest in the monies that are raised, eg sports teams raising funds for participation in European tournaments

- Getting students to contribute to bids themselves is hugely rewarding. They often use frank, uninhibited language, which we would not consider using to describe their situation. Don't be afraid to include direct quotes in your funding applications – funders often find these deeply impressive

- A student council is an excellent vehicle for involving a wide cross-section of interested and motivated students in fundraising. The home-school association is an equally powerful group to promote this work, and if representatives can be included from the student council so much the better

Setting
the Scene

 Getting
Started

 The Ten-Step
Model

 Fundraising
in Action

 Monitoring
and
Evaluating

 Tools/Further
Information

Monitoring and Evaluating

What are monitoring and evaluation?

Monitoring and evaluation are firmly established buzzwords in education.
They're also an important part of your fundraising work.

Monitoring is about judging the **progress** you are
making with your work.

Evaluation is concerned with the **success**
of your work and judging whether it has
been worthwhile.

Monitoring techniques

Monitoring should be done in close consultation with your fundraising development plan and is about gathering information on such things as:

- Whether research has been carried out
- Whether audits have been carried out as planned
- Whether applications have actually been made
- The results of applications
- The participation of students in projects
- Whether the project budget is being used in line with the application
- Whether you are making satisfactory progress towards funding targets
- Whether your overall plans are proceeding to schedule

Monitoring individual projects is important because you will often be asked by funders to provide information on such things as participation rates and budgeting. Keep scrupulous records of everything, including, where possible, participants' views on projects and before and after photographs to demonstrate progress.

Evaluation techniques

Evaluating involves looking at:

- Whether your overall fundraising work is bearing fruit
- Whether your individual projects are having the desired impact

Successful evaluation allows you to judge whether **alternative** strategies need to be used to make either individual projects or your overall work more effective.

Roles and responsibilities

Nobody should expect to carry out monitoring and evaluation alone. The fundraising coordinator should take an **overview** and have overall responsibility, but others may also be involved in the process:

- Evaluating the success of the school's fundraising may be carried out by the headteacher as part of the fundraising coordinator's annual performance review
- For individual projects, the day-to-day monitoring may be passed on to the designated project manager

Annual reports

It's important to produce short **annual reports** that summarise fundraising progress during the year. They could include details of:

- Funding applications made
- Successes
- Community links
- Other fundraising activities
- Progress with individual projects
- Priorities for the coming year

These reports should be shared with the senior management team, governors, other staff and perhaps parents/carers too. They can also provide an excellent basis for **annual reviews** of the fundraising coordinator, carried out with SMT or governors. By sharing this information widely, you will be sending the message that fundraising matters at your school.

Project reports

You will need to produce **project reports** for all individual projects when the work is complete. Many funders request these to make sure you are accountable for the money they have given you. Even if they don't, it's good practice to write them and send the funder a copy.

Project reports should be concise and to the point, containing:

- The aims of the project
- A report on what was done and whether the aims were met
- An overall evaluation of the success of the project, with reference to the intended outcomes and including participants' views on the success of the project
- A breakdown of how the money was spent
- A record of the outcomes of the project if this is possible (eg, students' work, photographs)

Looking to the future

As well as keeping an eye on what has been successful in the past, the fundraising coordinator should also look to the future and make plans for what is next.

Particularly important in this context is:

*   Keeping up to date with the latest funding opportunities
*   Discussing with school managers and staff details of any emerging priorities for the school. These should be built into the fundraising development plan, but only if there is time to address them on top of the existing priority areas or if others are shelved. They may have to wait until your next fundraising development plan is prepared

Once your fundraising work has settled down into a more predictable pattern, it's sensible to synchronise the production of the fundraising plan with whole school development planning.

'Recycling' applications

It's worth bearing in mind that any **unsuccessful** applications are not worthless just because one funder has rejected them. Funders sometimes offer guidance on why your application was not successful and this kind of information is invaluable. Alternatively, it may be that your project can be submitted to another funder without extensive alteration.

Keeping focused

R E M E M B E R

'It's easy to forget the importance of monitoring and evaluating your fundraising work – do not let the hectic nature of the job allow you to lose sight of these essential activities'

Setting
the Scene

 Getting
Started

 The Ten-Step
Model

 Fundraising
in Action

 Monitoring
and
Evaluating

 Tools/Further
Information

Tools/Further Information

Charitable status

It's well worth considering applying for **charitable status** for your 'friends of' or PTA group, as it allows you to apply to a wide range of educational trusts which are simply not available to you as a school alone. It also enables you to claim **gift aid** monies – worth at least 22p in the pound – on donations to your school, for example from parents or carers following a public appeal.

The process involves having a small group of people who are prepared to put themselves forward as officers of the charity, and the completion of some quite lengthy, but pretty straightforward forms. For more details contact the Charity Commission at www.charity-commission.gov.uk.

Note that church schools do not need to seek charitable status, as this is conferred through affiliation to the church.

Project summary template

Project title (snappy, concise, attractive):

Aims of the project ....

Who will benefit? ....

How many people will benefit? ....

How will they benefit? ....

How has the need been identified? ....

Who will be involved in the project and what will their roles be? ....

What is the budget for the project? ....

What is the timetable for the project? ....

How will the project be monitored? ....

How will the project be evaluated? ....

How will the impact of the project be sustained? ....

Example press release

ANYTOWN SCHOOL UNVEILS LANDMARK PROJECT

A local school is putting itself on the map thanks to an innovative project that will *insert details here*

The school is now approaching local business and the community to join with it in transforming the school for both its students and the wider community. There is a range of specific ways in which help is required and the school will be staging an information evening on *insert date and time* to unveil its exciting plans.

Headteacher *insert name*, said: 'This project will help put the school at the forefront of development in the field of *insert details here* but we will only be successful if we can gain the support of the local community. I appeal to everyone to get involved and play their part.'

For more details of the school's work, contact fundraising coordinator *insert name* on *insert contact details*.

Ends

Using buildings and grounds

Out-of-hours uses for school buildings

- Evening classes
- Choir/music group practice
- Training venue for businesses
- Launch venue for company community initiative
- Meeting rooms for community groups
- Venue for theatre performances
- School reunions/nostalgia evenings
- Art exhibitions
- Tea dances

Out-of-hours uses for school grounds

- Car boot sales
- Parking for a special event nearby
- Sports competitions
- Caravan rallies
- Community festival venue

71 fundraising ideas

If you are school fundraiser caught in a rut, try some of the following:

1. Seek a corporate sponsor to invest in an annual award for the student who tries hardest at school.

2. Ask local companies to sponsor items of equipment linked to their trade.

3. Ask a local computer supplier to donate refurbished machines to raise the profile of ICT among students and staff, in return for publicity.

4. Enter all competitions advertised in the education press and in flyers.

5. Organise a summer fête or autumn fair.

6. Stage a fashion show using students' designs and charge an entry fee.

7. Hold a sponsored walk with a theme, eg local history, spring flowers.

8. Approach ex-students, now in business, to become benefactors.

9. Organise a series of non-uniform days with a special theme.

10. Ask a local printer, publisher or newspaper to sponsor the school newsletter.

11. Invite a guest speaker with links to the school (eg a well-known local personality or media figure) to a cheese and wine evening for parents.

12. Ask parents to contribute a one-off extra to school funds.

13. Stage a table-top sale.

14. Invite a local garden centre to sponsor a flowerbed.

15. Request support from the local Chamber of Commerce.

16. Stage a staff review that students pay a small fee to watch.

17. Organise an auction of promises.

71 fundraising ideas

18. Collect cans and paper for recycling.

19. Organise a quiz night.

20. Publish a yearbook that depicts all students and staff and charge a fee for it.

21. Ask a computer software manufacturer to provide software for evaluation.

22. Ask a local or national newspaper to provide free copies to improve literacy.

23. Stage a talent show for students and staff.

24. Organise a lunchtime karaoke event for staff and students – guaranteed fun for some!

25. Organise a bucket collection of loose change.

26. Collect unwanted foreign currency.

27. Collect tokens for education products from supermarkets.

28. Organise a sponsored spell/mental arithmetic test.

29. Sponsor teachers to wear unconventional dress (!).

30. Stage an art exhibition with student works for sale.

31. Apply to professional bodies for research or special project grants.

32. Take an aerial photograph of the school with the students standing in line to make the date.

71 fundraising ideas

33. Use local authority equipment stores.

34. Apply to National Lottery funds.

35. Approach regional arts boards to stage an event.

36. Tap into LEA advisers' projects funds.

37. Apply for landfill tax grants for environmental improvements.

38. Investigate a partnership with Arts/Sports Council projects.

39. Enter company-sponsored community projects.

40. Link up with a local group to prepare a joint bid for a project, eg refurbishment of an out-of-use building.

41. Apply to educational trusts for grants.

42. Exploit governors' business contacts.

43. Organise a raffle or tombola.

44. Lay a line of 10p pieces from one football goal to another, inviting people from your local community to help score a goal!

45. Organise a cookery demonstration.

46. Ask a local music group to play in the school.

47. Make Christmas cards to sell.

48. Have a healthy food week where nutritious items are sold instead of sweets.

49. Ask a local football team to hold a soccer skills day.

50. Take a large whole-school photograph and invite bids from local companies to sponsor the display case.

51. Nurture a strong PTA who will be able to help with many of the above.

52. Stage a beauty evening.

53. Have a race night (simulated horse racing with betting).

54. Have a Greek night with plate smashing!

55. Arrange a barn dance.

56. Make a school calendar to sell.

71 fundraising ideas

57. Sell personalised sweatshirts, T-shirts, polo shirts etc.

58. Arrange bag-packing in a local supermaket.

59. Collect old clothes and shoes for recycling (20p per kilo paid).

60. Produce individual school photographs in-house.

61. Sell personalised stationery.

62. Stage a martial arts demonstration.

63. Shave a bearded teacher (pay per view only!)

64. Organise a duck race on a local stream.

65. Stage a plant sale.

66. Sell tea towels featuring students' artwork.

67. Photograph sports teams and the student council.

68. Carry out car-washing in the community.

69. Do a sponsored litter pick.

70. Organise a lunchtime disco.

71. Contact your LEA school travel plan coordinator to investigate funding opportunities for your school (£5,000 for primary schools and £10,000 for secondary schools on offer to schools who write and implement a plan).

Books and directories

Schools Funding Guide by N. Eastwood, A. Mountfield and L. Walker
Published by Directory of Social Change, 2001
Includes extensive guidance on funders for the education sector

School Fundraising in England: A Directory of Social Change Research Report
by A. Mountfield and N. Eastwood
Published by Directory of Social Change, 2000
The results of the most comprehensive survey ever completed into fundraising in England.

The Luck Factor: The Scientific Study of the Lucky Mind by R. Wiseman
Published by Arrow, 2003
Shows you how to be lucky with your fundraising work and your personal life – an amazing piece of research that could change your life.

CDs and online resources

Grant-making Trusts CD-ROM
Contains information on more than 4,250 trusts who between them give out over £1 billion a year (£120 + VAT; for details see www.dsc.org.uk or telephone 020 7391 4800)

www.funderfinder.org.uk
Develops and distributes software to help individuals and not-for-profit organisations in the UK to identify charitable trusts that might give them money. Its website provides access to a Groups in Need search facility of over 4,500 funders (£150 + VAT; see website for details or telephone 0113 243 2966)

www.trustfunding.org.uk
Over 4,000 up-to-date trusts, available via the internet, with emails advising of updates to the site. Available on a subscription basis from the Directory of Social Change (£120 + VAT; for details see www.dsc.org.uk or telephone 020 7391 4800)

www.fundraising.co.uk
Free information for UK charity and non-profit fundraisers

www.lotterygoodcauses.org.uk
Latest information on how to get National Lottery funding, news on the organisations that distribute lottery money, and case studies of projects that the lottery has funded in the past

Newsletters and magazines

Practical Funding for Schools
The best periodical on fundraising, published by Step Forward Publishing 11 times a year. This 16-page magazine contains a wealth of practical advice on fundraising as well as up to date listings of the latest funding opportunities (£49.50 annually; tel. 01926 420046, www.practicalfunding.com).

School Financial Management
A 12-page newsletter, published by Optimus Publishing 10 times a year and aimed mainly at bursars and school finance managers. It contains regular articles on funding and a round-up of the latest funding opportunities (£65 primary schools, £95 secondary schools annually; tel. 0845 450 5404, www.optimuspub.co.uk).

Contact addresses

**International Resource Centre
for Schools and Colleges
(European funding)**
27 Salmon Grove
University of Hull
Hull HU6 7RX
Tel. 01482 305150

Specialist Schools Trust
16th Floor
Millbank Tower
21-24 Millbank
London SW1P 4QP
Tel. 020 7802 2300
www.specialistschools.org.uk

Specialist Schools Designation Team
Department for Education & Skills
2F Area F Mowden Hall
Staindrop Road
Darlington DL3 9BG
Download the application form and guidance
from www.standards.dfes.gov.uk/specialistschools

**Dixons City Technology College
(contact for Software production)**
Tony Hosker, Interactive Learning Ltd, Dixons CTC
Ripley Street, West Bowling
Bradford BD5 7RR
Tel. 01274 220738
www.interactive-learning.info

Your local voluntary action bureau is likely to be an excellent source of support for your fundraising work. They often allow access to electronic funding databases, can advise on making applications, and have useful local contacts. For contact details see the Yellow Pages or your local library.

Acknowledgements

Brin Best
I am grateful to the staff and students at Settle High School and Community College, where I learnt much about the role of the school fundraising coordinator. My ideas on school fundraising have been shaped by my work with Doncaster and Hull LEAs and their schools, and with many individual schools in other areas. I have found Sue Marsden's and Louise Germaney's ideas on school fundraising especially stimulating. Much of my early work involved fundraising for environmental projects, and I am indebted to my mother from whom I learnt much during my vacation work at the Stockport Council for Voluntary Service.

Ken Dunn
I am grateful to the staff and students of Royston High School with whom I enjoyed ten very successful years and learnt a great deal. I am particularly indebted to John Wilkinson, Pat Newman and Bob Taylor who encouraged me in this work. My heartfelt thanks go to Karen, Thomas and Katie for their love and support.

Ros Baynes, Linda Edge and Gill O'Donnell provided helpful comments on an earlier draft of the book.

About the authors

Brin Best

Brin Best BSc, PGCE, FRGS, FMA, MCIJ is managing director of Innovation *for* Education Ltd, an education training, publishing and consultancy company based in Yorkshire. Brin has 16 years' experience fundraising for schools and charitable projects. He led the fundraising for his school's bid for technology college status. His company works in partnership with schools and LEAs to help schools maximise their income from external sources. He edits *School Financial Management*, has spoken widely on fundraising for schools, and chaired several national conferences on the subject.

Ken Dunn

Ken Dunn BSc, PGCE, FRGS, FMA, assistant headteacher at a large secondary school in Sheffield, won the Royal Geographic Society's Ordnance Survey Award, 2005 in recognition of 'excellence in teaching geography in secondary education'. Keen on environmental matters – local and global – Ken has developed many innovative projects which have won national awards. He writes and speaks widely on fundraising for schools and is a regular keynote speaker at national funding conferences. Ken's royalties for this book will go to the Malealea Development Trust to assist a remarkable community in Lesotho, southern Africa with whom he has worked since 2000.

Order Form

Your details

Name _____

Position _____

School _____

Address _____

_____

_____

Telephone _____

Fax _____

E-mail _____

VAT No. (EC only) _____

Your Order Ref _____

Please send me:

		No. copies
Fundraising for Schools	Pocketbook	☐
_____	Pocketbook	☐
_____	Pocketbook	☐
_____	Pocketbook	☐
_____	Pocketbook	☐

Order by Post
Teachers' Pocketbooks
Laurel House, Station Approach
Alresford, Hants. SO24 9JH UK

Order by Phone, Fax or Internet
Telephone: +44 (0)1962 735573
Facsimile: +44 (0)1962 733637
E-mail: sales@teacherspocketbooks.co.uk
Web: www.teacherspocketbooks.co.uk